Camping !

Horlie
Hyde

Hello Mudder!

Special thanks to Daisy (Chuck) Zehner

While the incidents in this book did happen, some of the names and personal characteristics of some of the individuals have been changed. Any resulting resemblance to persons living or dead is entirely coincidental and unintentional.

Book design by the Troy Book Makers
Printed in the United States of America
The Troy Book Makers • Troy, New York • thetroybookmakers.com

To order additional copies of this title, contact your favorite local bookstore or visit www.tbmbooks.com

ISBN: 978-1-61468-1908

Hello Mudder!

Herbie's memorable summer adventure

A Tiny, Teenie, Weenie Memoir

BY

Herb Hyde

To begin with let me paraphrase a famous song. *Summer-time and the camping is easy.* Many people look back with fondness at their sleep away camp experiences as a child or teenager: Fishing, swimming, canoeing, hiking, learning survival skills in the great outdoors. Making lifelong friendships, or in some cases enemies, if you were bullied or if you were a bully yourself.

You might remember your counselor spinning tales around the camp fire and scaring you half to death, or helping you deal with that squiggly worm while learning to fish. How he patted you on the back when you finished making your first Indian bracelet in arts and crafts or comforted you when you scraped your knee sliding into home plate.

Your mom knew when you came home: tan, taller and seemingly happier than when you left that she had made the right decision letting you go-- even though she had some serious reservations in the beginning. Now she looked forward to you going next year as much as you did.

Now let me tell you my story.

I was so bored that cloudy summer day walking along Fourth Street that I just stared down at the craggy, crooked lines, dividing the crumbling cement sidewalk. Looking up after dawdling along for quite a while, I noticed a female mannequin staring out the window at me with her steely blue eyes. Sensuously draped over her shoulder was an amber colored, golden fox cape. I just stood there mesmerized, watching this inanimate being as though she was a real person.

Ding! The sound of the door opening startled me back to reality. A well-dressed elderly woman, her silver hair perfectly coifed, approached me with a friendly, welcoming smile. The scent of her expensive perfume and the richness of the furs I saw lining her shop became etched into my brain.

"Hi, Young man. What's your name?"

"My name is Herbie."

"Would you like to come inside and see more of the things we have?"

Confused, I thought for a moment, "Should I go inside with a stranger?" Although it did look interesting in there with all those coats and furs lining the walls. "OK", I said to her, as she ushered me in to meet her smiling husband, a robust older gentleman in a dark pinstripe suit and brilliant red tie. His half-rimmed glasses were situated near the end of his elongated nose. His dark brown eyes stared probingly into mine, trying to analyze what was going on in my head. Those probing eyes made me feel uncomfortable. I quickly began nervously staring at the floor in order to ease my discomfort. However, when I did return his stare I noticed his thinning hair, similar to Grandpa Davenport's. I then began to feel a little more at ease as he grasped my hand and shook it until he almost lifted me off the ground with his enthusiasm.

They had been looking for me: a poor kid in tattered clothes, who would become their "fresh air kid" this year. I would soon be shipped off to Camp Piteous located in the Catskill Mountains near the New York and New Jersey border. I would be pampered with some new clothes and Samsonite suitcases to be used as props while the local newspaper snapped a picture of this lucky kid up in Prospect Park. In the picture I looked like a stick figure with scrawny arms, a brush cut and big ears--holding two suitcases that were almost as tall as I was.

The Bockmen's, wealthy furriers had donated money each year to send a needy, deserving Troy youth to the beautiful, sleep away camp utilized mostly for inner New York City kids. After moving from Queens ten years earlier to Troy, they began partncring with the Troy Boys Club in this altruistic cause. It made them feel good to give some of their wealth back to the community in some thoughtful manner. It had brought great joy to them and to many deserving kids in the past.

However, they had not yet met, Herbie! They didn't realize that I had rarely been away from home and that I didn't handle separation from my family very well. I had spent two horror-filled weeks a few years earlier at Camp Barker. If only they had known how unable to cope I would be when I arrived at camp and that I really didn't want to go; they probably wouldn't have sponsored me. But now I was their pride and joy! I would be treated like royalty for the few weeks leading up to my departure. When I stopped by for a visit they would take me out for something to eat at Pafundi's Luncheonette on Grand Street, or offer me chocolates from the Fanny Farmer store on River Street reserved for their preferred customers.

Soon the big day arrived. I vividly remember that I hardly slept the night before, tossing and turning endlessly, trying to figure out how to finagle my way out of going. But I couldn't. I couldn't disappoint Ma. She was so excited about me being picked to go to this special camp. Earlier in the week she was having coffee with Winnie Koch and Helen Howard and was just beaming about me to both of them. I glumly sat nestled into my usual corner seat near the stove. My stomach was churning with apprehension. I was petrified about going on this trip. But, I was unable to tell Ma my feelings. How could I now after listening to what they were saying.

"I'm so proud of Herbie being picked to go Helen."

"Well I don't blame you, Mable." Helen said. "It's quite an honor. Dom Greco told Walt that he was competing against dozens of other deserving kids at the club. In fact, the club had actually picked another kid from the Ahearn Apartments to go. But Mrs. Bockmen had insisted that they wanted Herbie to go instead. They must have seen something very special in Herbie, Mable."

Ma's eyes just lit up when she heard that and said. "He is a special little boy, a handful at times, but special." All three of them laughed at that as I cringed.

"I'm totally screwed now," I thought. "Why did I have stop in front of their darn store."

Ma gave me a big hug as I stood sadly in the doorway, hoping she would notice. She didn't. Instead she just told me to write her if I got lonely. She had packed some kids stationary into my brother Sonny's old, duffle bag, along with several pairs of underwear, polo shirts, shorts and dungarees the Bockmen's had bought for me. She also packed a new tooth brush and comb as well as a bag lunch: baloney sandwich, peanut butter cookies and potato chips.

"Don't you forget to brush your teeth, Herbie!"

"I won't Ma."

"And, try not to wet your bed! You have been doing really well lately."

"I'll try my best, Ma. I promise" The horrible memories of sleeping on those empty, wet cotton ticks at Camp Barker flooded my mind. "Boy," I thought. "I hope they don't have cotton ticks at this camp."

It was 6:30 in the morning and within minutes Dom Greco was ringing the doorbell. I soon headed off to what I thought was going to be my worst nightmare--three weeks of pure hell. Dom drove me down to the Bus Station at Ferry and Fourth where he handed me over to my counselor, Joe. He would have the responsibility to watch over me and several other kids from Albany, Ravena and some nameless hick town located in the heart of the Catskill Mountains until we reached our destination. I thought I would be riding in one of those cushy Greyhound buses I'd seen parked there while roaming the city with my buddies. Nope! Instead we had to ride in a rickety, yellow school bus on a bumpy four hour trip that seemed like it took four days.

I never saw so many trees in my all life and wondered: "Boy! I bet Dad could make a fortune cutting them down. He'd never run out of work. Hum, I wonder if he knows about this place." I made a mental note to tell him when I got back home.

Hurtling up and down winding mountain roads was getting tiring and scary. I closed my eyes most of the time because I got so scared looking down at the craggy ravines below. It was on this trip that I developed the habit of praying whenever I travel. Eventually we started going past small towns, farms and a place called Port Jarvis which was located along the Delaware River. The one thing I noticed about the river was that it was bone dry, so I asked Joe why.

"Well, Herbie, It's been a very hot, dry summer. Actually, we are in the midst of a drought."

"Ok," I said. I surmised that drought and dry probably meant the same thing. I remember Ma complaining about how hot it was, and how we had hardly any rain to Winnie, while sitting on our front porch on a stifling night a week earlier.

Shortly after passing Port Jarvis we headed back uphill for a while longer before entering a wide driveway and into a paved parking lot. At the end of parking lot stood a large, L-shaped, wood building with a low pitched roof, and a large brick chimney located in the middle of it. The building was surrounded by large, well-kept lawns and colorful flowered shrub beds near the office. The office was the smaller section of the building which gave the facility its L shape. Within minutes of stopping near the front door, our slovenly bus driver, who looked like a character from the movie Deliverance, pried open the front door, using the squeaky metal handle that rattled like it would fall off at any minute. As I was walking by he appeared to be glaring at me. But suddenly he began to smile, which high-lighted his odorous, semi-toothless mouth. I held my breath as I quickly hopped off the bus.

It was about 12:05 when Joe brought us into the office to check in. We were soon met by a smiling lady named Mrs. Kaplan. She checked our permission slips then checked our names off her attendance sheet. She then told us, in a not so friendly voice, to sit on a hard wooden bench and wait for the head counselor. Sitting there I felt my stomach grumbling and realized I hadn't eaten the lunch Ma had packed for me. Now I was starving and reached into my sack and pulled out my lunch. Nobody seemed to notice me eating my bologna sandwich, but when I started crunching loudly on my potato chips, all heck broke out.

"Camper! Stop that right this minute," yelled a tall brown haired guy with a brush cut. He was wearing a uniform consisting of black sneakers, white gym socks, tan shorts and a pressed tan shirt with a green name tag stitched onto the pocket. It read: Sid, Tessler--Head Counselor.

"Oh, boy" I thought to myself. "This ain't good."

"You don't eat meals in this office. Lunch is in the mess hall at 12:30, sharp!"

Mess-hall. Was I in the service now?

"But, I'm starved, sir," I blurted, while hastily chomping down my last chip.

"The first lesson you will learn here is that there are rules, and you have to follow them. Do you understand?"

Now I was getting upset. Tired and overstimulated by my new surroundings, I foolishly argued like the small eight year old brat I was. "I don't care about your stupid rules. I'm hungry and I'm going to eat right now!"

Just as I was about to take another bite of my sandwich, Sid ripped it out of my hand and told me to stand in the corner near the desk until lunch was called. That's when I really took a tantrum and threw myself on the floor, crying and yelling for my mother. "I want to go home, I don't want to be here and you can't make me stay."

"Get off the floor right now," yelled counselor, Sid. I refused and continued crying and screaming for Ma as dozens of kids began streaming by the office door with quizzical looks on their face. They were all headed for the mess hall. Suddenly, I heard a door slam shut down the hall and rapid footsteps pounding on the weathered pine floor.

"What is all this commotion, Sid?" Said Mr. Grouse the camp's director.

"I caught this new camper sneaking a sandwich right before lunch. He got sassy with me and wouldn't stop eating, so I took his sandwich away. That's when he took a tantrum and threw himself on the floor."

"I was hungry," I screamed from my prone position on the floor, as these two huge ogres hovered over me.

"I hope he is not going to be a problem, Sid. I can't tolerate any problems like we had last year with that kid from Queens running away. We should have let him have what he wanted. It almost cost me my job."

"Hum," I thought to myself. I listened intently between screams, flailing my arms and legs while they huddled nearby, whispering about the best course of action to take with me. Did they want to relive the drama of the previous year? They must have thought they were out of ear shot, but they were not. I was able to hear their muffled concerns and filed those concerns in my noggin for future use, if need be.

Soon they came back to where I was lying on the floor and agreed to let me finish my sandwich.

"Here's the deal," Sid, Said. "You can finish your sandwich, but you have to go into the mess hall with all the other kids in order to do it."

I reluctantly agreed and followed them in. As we walked through the arched entrance to the mess hall I could see dozens of kids standing patiently in line with their trays, waiting to be served a host of interesting looking food items: Salads, soup, burgers and assorted premade sandwiches and desserts. Wow! I had never seen such a variety of food in one place before. Smelling the hearty aroma of sizzling beef, I couldn't resist. I threw my unfinished sandwich in the garbage can near the counter and ordered a burger, along with some macaroni salad, large chocolate milk and a bowl of rice pudding.

I sat on one of the large wooden benches next to a black kid from Queens. He was about three inches taller than me, and tough looking. He had a jagged scar on his chin and tiny ears that looked like miniature, black cauliflowers. His cropped, kinky black hair reminded me of Andy Joules. He just sat there ignoring me when I tried to strike up a conversation.

"Hi, I'm Herbie. What's your name?"

He wouldn't say at first, but after a few moments he finally mumbled, "My name is Ray Pell. Hey, what's all that commotion you had in the office?"

"Oh, it was nothing." I said. "I was just eating my baloney sandwich when that big goofus, what's his name, ripped it out of my hand for no reason. Then he started yelling at me like he was my boss and told me I had to take orders from him and stuff. I got scared when he shoved me on the floor," I fibbed. I didn't want to tell this kid I was a little baby crying for my mommy.

"Sid is a big Jerk," chimed Ray, my new best friend. Apparently, Ray had several run-ins with Sid the previous summer at camp, so anything negative I spouted, fed into Ray's preconceived prejudices of counselor, Sid. Ray and I become best buddies for most of my three week sentence in purgatory.

After lunch, Sid walked in to make his usual lecture to the new campers. There were a total of 30 new kids replacing the 30 kids who had left to go home that morning before we arrived. The camp had a staggered enrollment. Some kids had a two week stay, while others would be there for three weeks like Ray and me. Moments before he addressed us, Sid dismissed the kids whom had been there from the previous two weeks. They were all allowed to go down to the lake for swimming or canoeing or out to the barn to do arts and crafts or work out in the gym. That huge, red building contained: a boxing ring, punching bags and a basketball court, as-well-as, locker rooms and arts and crafts rooms.

After Ray and the other kids left Sid started his spiel: Each morning at 6:30 we would get up at the sound of reveille, played over the p.a. system, go to the bathroom, brush our teeth, make our beds, and get dressed then head outside where two privileged kids raised the American Flag. We would then head back inside for breakfast in the mess hall. During breakfast, a deserving kid selected by the counselors each week, would read the morning announcements, then play music like a disk jockey. (Cool job for a deserving kid)

Once Sid was done yakking, he led us into a large room off the mess hall. At the entrance to the bunk house were two large bathrooms on either side of the room. Then there were rows and rows of beds on each side of the room, and a series of open wooden cabinets over the head of each bed. Those cabinets were used to store our clothes. At the foot of the unmade beds were sheets, blankets, pillows and pillow cases. Sid assigned each of us to a bed. He then began giving us more rules we had to follow. But first he gave us an ominous warning.

"If any of you wet the bed you had better tell me now!" He then cocked his eyebrow in an intimidating manner that suggested that if you did wet the bed you were in deep trouble. Even though I had not had an accident in weeks, I began to feel scared that I might. I didn't need more dread in my life at this time so I just closed my mind to that fear and said nothing. I didn't want the embarrassment of having to admit that I wet the bed in front of my camp mates.

Sid then began to explain how to make our beds properly. First you had to put on the sheets, making hospital corners, which sounded very complicated to me. He started showing us how by making the first bed next to the bathroom. Ironically, that would end up being my bed. He then had each of us attempt to do it. Most kids got it down pretty good after a few attempts. Me? Not so much.

"Mr. Hyde! What is your problem? I have shown you how to make those corners three times already. No more. If they are not done properly tomorrow morning, you will not be able to participate in the morning activities until you do it right!"

"Jeez No pressure there," I thought.

"Ok, boss" I spouted back sarcastically.

"Watch your mouth" Insidious Sid chimed back.

"Yes sir." I saluted back.

What an auspicious start to my first day at camp. Things could only get better.

Of course I woke up the next morning drenched. I wet the bed and now I would have hell to pay. Sid came into the room on our first morning there and like the drill sergeant he was, immediately noticed my predicament and began haranguing me for not telling him I was a bed wetter. I really wasn't. I just had this one little accident.

"Why didn't you tell me you wet the bed," Sid yelled.

"I don't!" I yelled back in my defense. "It was just an accident. I'm sorry," I said.

"Sorry doesn't make it here." Sid lectured back. "Now we have to get a new mattress and put a plastic cover over it. Go into the bathroom and get cleaned up. I think you're going to a real problem here." That's when I threw myself on the floor and started to cry hysterically.

"Stop the crying." Sid insisted. But I couldn't. I just wanted my mother.

"I want to go home!" I cried over and

over. Now Sid was beside himself, not being able to calm me down in front of all the other campers who watched with fascination at what was going on. Some with smirks on their faces, probably thinking I was a sissy. Would I have to suffer their taunts now? I wanted out in the worst way. Remembering what Sid and the camp director discussed when I got there the day before, gave me a glimmer of hope that I could finagle a way to go home.

However, that didn't happen. Instead they decided to appease me and gave me the best job at camp: Having me make the morning announcements, instead of a more deserving camper. That way they could keep an eye on me and not worry that I would cause more problems. I felt like Robin Williams in "Good Morning Viet Nam." I really felt important now. Ironically, I never wet the bed again.

During the second week of camp, a huge hurricane barreled up the east coast. Hurricane Hazel wreaked havoc on the northeast, causing tremendous flooding and damage to communities along the Delaware River, especially Port Jarvis. It rained so much that worms were floating on top of the grass at camp, and campers were stuck inside for almost an entire week until the storm subsided. I began to adjust much better as the weeks passed by. I would hang out and eat lunch and dinner with my buddy Ray. He kind of protected me from anyone who might try to bully me. It was actually fun watching as bats that had been sequestered in the attic of the mess hall, would dive bomb us in the dining room each morning. They would barely miss campers, who ducked to avoid getting a bat stuck in their hair. Remember those old urban legends about bats. I'm not sure, but I think the storm knocked their circadian clocks out of whack.

Every Wednesday night was fight night at Camp. My buddy, Ray fought the first two weeks and pummeled his opponents in the round robin tournament. He was the only undefeated fighter and would vie for the shiny gold trophy awarded to the best boxer tonight. Each week the counselors would select sixteen kids to fight in eight two round fights. The intent was to have each kid in camp get a taste of what it was like to be a boxer, and learn to defend himself. Each and every week I kept my fingers crossed that I wouldn't be selected and luckily I wasn't. I think the counselors didn't want to force me to fight at first, because they were afraid I'd have another meltdown. However, this last week they had a hideous change of heart and insisted I fight. (I think deep down they wanted to make me pay for being such a pain)

"Ok, Hydie, it's your turn to fight tonight. You're fighting Ray in the last bout." Said Insidious, Sid; a demonic smile on his puss.

I was scared to death but refused to take my usual tantrum. I didn't want the other campers to think I was a coward. However, I prayed that somehow the building would get struck by lightning and the power would go out before my fight. What a cruel injustice; having my best friend kick the snot out of me so he could win some stinking, shiny trophy.

There was a delay in getting the fights started because dinner had run late due to a minor grease fire in the kitchen. So instead of starting at seven they started at seven thirty. Ironically, my buddy Ray would be forced to fight two fights tonight. One fight against Jimmy Hackney, the only guy with just one loss, and after whooping him, which he did; He would have to finish the night of by whooping me in the final fight of the night. (How sinister these counselors turned out to be).

My stomach was churning as each fight moved along and time drew nearer for my demise. However, unlike in previous weeks most of the fights went the distance. Outside you could hear thunder and see lightning from a residual pop-up storm; a hangover from Hurricane Hazel, I think. In fact the lights began flickering off and on a few times around eight thirty, causing the ref to delay the start of the seventh fight of the night for several minutes. I was so nervous worrying about this fight that I had to run to the bathroom located in the back of the barn several times to pee. I guess my bladder was more nervous than I was. After the third trip to the john, in comes Sid to check on me.

"What are you doing in here Hydie?" (Boy how I hate being called, Hydie)

"I have to pee."

"Well make it quick because you're not getting out of this fight, hear me?"

"Yea, I hear you," I sadly lamented.

I soon slumped back into my seat at the back of the arena awaiting my fate, as the second to last fight was finishing up between blond Eddie Riley and Hector Dominique. Now I was really getting scared as Sid ran over and frantically began forcing gloves onto my hands. He was like a demon and I couldn't understand why. The bell sounded to end the second to last fight, and within of couple minutes the ref was holding up Eddie Riley's hand. Eddie then proceeded to proudly prance around the ring with his gloved hands held high, as though he'd just won the world 'scrawny weight' championship.

"Oh boy," I thought, as Mr. Grouse, the ringside announcer, grabbed the microphone to quickly call the last fight.

"In this corner we have undefeated, Ray Pell!"

Ray then jitterbugged around the ring as though he was Sugar Ray Robinson, instead of Ray Pell: amateur nine year old. All the kids in the crowd roared their approval. It was beginning to feel like the Romans and the lions, and I was about to be thrown to the lions.

Without warning, a sweaty hand grabbed my forearm tightly and began pulling me out of my seat.

"Come on Hydie, get your scrawny butt out of this chair and get in the ring," insidious Sid callously whispered in my ear.

"Stop it you idiot!" I screamed back. I think everyone in the room must have heard me. Unrelenting, Sid started dragging me toward the ring with my stiffened legs and sneakers scraped across the hard wood floor. Time was clicking away as I approached the ring. Ironically Mr. Grouse peered down at me with a stunned look on his puss. I think he was beginning to wonder what Sid was up too.

He warily watched as Sid dragged me toward the ring. Sid looked like a storm trooper dragging a peaceful protester to jail at some anti-war rally.

Kaboom! Just as Sid began shoving me by my butt up the stairs to the ring, a lightning bolt struck right outside the gym. Kids began screaming as the lights flickered and went out for a good ten minutes. The counselors were busy trying to console the frightened campers, encouraging them to stay in their seats so they wouldn't trip over someone or something. In the meantime I just sat on the ring steps holding my head in my gloved hands to block out the noise and hoping the lights would come on soon. I was scared to death when the lights blew out. However, I was even more scared about what was going too happened to me when they came back on.

By the time the lights finally came back on it was well after our 9 pm curfew. I remained seated on the steps while the counselors and Mr. Grouse discussed what to do. Luckily, they decided to cancel the last fight, much to the dismay of insidious Sid. Instead they took a few minutes to hand out the awards. My buddy Ray Pell received his gold trophy, holding it over his head as he proudly pranced around the ring. I just sighed with relief as Sid angrily pulled my gloves off and sent me immediately back to my bunk. I slept like a baby that night.

The last two days of camp went by without any more incidents or turmoil. Saturday morning we packed up our belongings, had our final oatmeal breakfast, said our goodbyes and were then herded onto several yellow school buses. Each bus had a chaperon assigned to it. They had the responsibility for getting us home safely. As my bus slowly began pulling away, a cadre of counselors standing outside the buses waved good bye to their favorite campers, many of whom were hanging out the windows with tears in their eyes. You see most of the campers had a wonderful time at camp, while a few, like, myself--not so much. I quietly stared out the window as Mrs. Kaplan waved goodbye, while insidious Sid just seemed to glare at me as we drove by.

Our bus quickly hurtled down the mountain as the sun radiantly flickered between the towering pines that lined the road. We soon reached Port Jarvis and I was astounded by what I saw. Instead of a bone dry river bed; I saw a raging river and several flooded homes and businesses lining the river. I also saw pitched roofs lying by the shore with no house to be found. Apparently some of the homes had been washed away downstream and all that was left were their roofs. What a scary, sad sight.

It took close to two hours before we reached New York City, slowly creeping through New Jersey as huge sky scrapers appeared in the distance. I was amazed at the sight because I had never been to the city and had only seen pictures of it. The most prominent building was the Empire State building which towered over the rest. What a spectacular site to see firsthand. My only recollection of that building was when I saw King Kong hanging off it while swatting at airplanes during one of our escapades sneaking into Proctor's Theater.

The traffic was bumper to bumper as we approached the Lincoln Tunnel. Boy that was a dank, dark and scary place. I prayed that we would get out of there quickly. Eventually we did exit the tunnel to the sounds of taxi's constantly honking their horns and throngs of people bustling along the street, some talking to them-selves.

Soon we pulled into a large enclosed bus terminal, the first stop in my day-long journey home. Randy, my chaperone, quickly came over and put his hand of my shoulder.

"Grab your stuff, quick. We have to catch the next subway to Grand Central, or you might miss the train back to Troy."

Scared to death, I grabbed Randy's hand as we hustled through a crowd, down a set of stairs to a smelly, tiled platform where Randy then clanged two gold coins into the slot of a turnstile. He then had me crawl under it because I wasn't strong enough to push through it, much to the chagrin of the subway attendant. We raced to the subway car and squeezed aboard just as the doors began to close. With me safely aboard with him, Randy, breathed a sigh of relief.

We clattered along on screeching electrified rails, as the subway car's doors rattled dangerously beside us. I held on for dear life as we hurtled through dark tunnels and flickering lights, finally reaching our destination as the conductor announced:

"Grand Central Station, last stop!"

As soon as we exited the car, Randy pushed me toward another set of stairs that led down to the waiting train that would spirit me back to Troy.

"Quick, Herbie! Hurry or we're going to miss it."

He grabbed my hand again and pulled me quickly down the marbled steps as fast as my little legs would go. At times it felt like I was flying down the stairs as I desperately grasped my brother, Sonny's duffle bag. We made it just in time as Randy handed me off to the conductor, gave him my ticket, which the conductor punched and handed back to me.

"Please make sure that he gets off at Troy," Randy told the conductor, a jovial black man with a big belly, mustache, horn rimmed glassed and a gray conductor's cap that highlighted his smiling brown eyes.

"I will take good care of him," He told Randy, as he ushered me to a window seat right next to his station.

"You stay there young man until we get you home, Ok?"

"Yes sir I told him." I had complete faith that this jovial man would take good care of me."

Looking out of my grime streaked window, I waved to Randy who was smiling at me and waved back. He was actually a nice guy who didn't seem to judge me the way that insidious Sid had. I could feel my body finally relax as the conductor made one last announcement.

"Last call," The conductor bellowed. "We're going to Kingston, Albany and Troy, all aboard!"

Within a few seconds the train slowly lumbered forward through a darkened tunnel, steam from the powerful engine rushing past my window like angry clouds desperately searching for sunlight. We quickly began rising from the bowels of this art deco metropolis into bright sunshine, as the wheels of this iconic train echoed off the walls of the concrete tunnel that encased the gritty nether world we were rapidly exiting: clickity-clack, clickity-clack, clickity-clack, hummed the wheels in a symphony of sounds that would eventually become a soothing ode to the beauty of the Hudson River valley we would soon traverse.

Exhausted by the stress of my journey home, I fell asleep as we approached Albany.

"Wake up young man, wake up." The conductor, nudged. "We will be home soon."

Still groggy from my prolonged nap, I quickly recognized we were in South Troy and rapidly heading toward the Ferry Street tunnel where I had often played chicken with oncoming trains.

"Hum," I thought. "I wonder if the guys are waiting to play chicken with my train."

Exiting the tunnel the train slowed to a crawl, passed by State Street, then edged its way toward Broadway and our own, beautiful 'Grand Central (Union) Station'. What a comforting site to behold. Seeing that magnificent building on my left, and my sister Dorothy waving at me with delight, with a huge welcoming smile on her face. The train shuddered, then lurched to an abrupt stop, as clouds of steam snorted from the nostrils of this magnificent, black beast.

"How was camp, Herbie?" Dorothy asked.

"It was great!" I lied.

"Ma will be so happy to see you." Dorothy said.

When I opened the door, there stood Ma in her familiar, print dress and apron and a smile on her face. I quickly fell into her outstretched arms and felt that I was finally home, safe, loved and at peace.

"You must have had a great time, Herbie?" Ma said. "You never wrote."

That was true, I hadn't written her. So I guess she figured I was ok. However, I didn't want to bother her with the minor details now.

"They made me the morning DJ at camp, Ma"

"That's great, Herbie." Ma, beamed.

"I'm glad you had a great time. Did you take anymore swimming lessons?"

"Not really, Ma. We had a lot of rain so we were in the gym a lot."

"Oh, yes that was quite a hurricane we had. I was really getting worried. But I assumed you were safe because nobody ever contacted us."

It was then that I gave her some of the details about the trip: learning how to make my bed, seeing roofs lying on the river bank, fighting for the boxing championship but having the storm short circuit it.

Of course I didn't tell her about my being a coward, or how I wet the bed, and how I took a couple minor tantrums. Everything was good, right?

"Boy I can't wait to tell Mrs. Bockmen about my trip, Ma."

Well you will have to wait until Monday because they are closed now for the weekend."

"Ok, Ma."

The weekend quickly passed and when Monday arrived I was itching to tell the Bockmen's about my great time at camp. I knew they would be impressed that I had been assigned the important job as DJ. I rushed through my breakfast of scrambled pullet eggs, toast and hot chocolate.

"Ma, I'm going downtown to visit the Bockmen's then maybe up to the park to play baseball with the guys."

"Ok Herbie, but make sure your back in time for lunch. I'm making bologna salad and Campbell's tomato soup."

"I will Ma."

It wasn't quite ten o'clock yet (The time the Bockmen's store opened) when I left the house. To kill some time, I decided to go into Union Station and walk through the tunnels where we often played. It was so much fun playing there, especially in the winter because we could get out of the cold and nobody bothered us, unless we angered some travelers--then we were kicked out.

It was around 10:15 when I exited the tunnel onto the boarding platform, just in time to see the 10:05 Laurention Express chugging out of the station and heading for Montreal.

Soon I was ambling my way down Fourth Street, excited about seeing the Bockmen's so I could tell them about my three week adventure. It was starting to get steamy outside. Apparently we were in the midst of another heat wave. The bell dinged as I opened the door and I soon felt cool air cascading across my face. I was all smiles as I approached the counter where Mrs. Bockmen was standing with her back to the door. She was in the midst of brushing off a mink coat before putting it into cold storage. The storage door was open and I could see Mr. Bockmen in the background stacking some boxes.

"Hi!" I gleefully shouted. "I'm back from camp."

Mrs. Bockmen abruptly turned around and angrily glared at me, her jaws were tightly clenched as though she was in pain. The welcoming smile she had when we first met had morphed into an ugly scowl of disdain. I was totally confused and wondered why.

"What's the matter Mrs. Bockmen?" I meekly implored.

"What's the matter? What's the matter?" she angrily screamed. "You have a nerve to ask that question!"

Now I was totally confused and a bit scared.

"George! Get out here now. I want you to tell him what the matter is," She yelled.

Within a few seconds, Mr. Bockmen stood hovering over the counter like a seven foot ogre, glaring down at me over his half-rimmed glasses. His dark brown eyes now appeared green to me, with the same red tinged, Satonic stare I remembered from Richie Spooner when use to he terrorize me. Now I was really scared, but still didn't understand why they were acting like this.

"Get out of my store and don't come back! We're ashamed of what you did. You embarrassed us with your behavior at Camp Piteous. We got nothing but bad reports from your counselor. We will never sponsor you again."

"But, I didn't do anything wrong," I cried with tears welling in my eyes. "I was homesick and missed my Ma."

"That is no excuse for your behavior. You wet the bed, you took tantrums, and you avoided participating in all the activities they provided, including learning how to box."

"But sir," I pleaded. "I didn't do it on purpose."

"It's too late for excuses now. Out, out," he shouted without one ounce of compassion for me.

He angrily pointed toward the door, as I sadly backed away with tears rolling down my cheeks and my heart broken. Was I that bad, I wondered, as I slowly walked home? How could they treat me this way: Fresh air kid, chocolates from Fanny Farmer, new clothes, Samsonite, suite cases used as props? Ma was so proud of me when I went, now she would be so disappointed in me if she found out. I never told her what happened that day. Instead I told her that I went down to the store and thanked them for sponsoring me.

Well I guess insidious, Sid got the last laugh, while I cried.